52 Motivational Quotations for Salespeople

One for every week of the year

Tom Cruz

ISBN: 0692359338
ISBN-13: 9780692359334

ACKNOWLEDGMENTS

I'd like to thank the first Sales Managers I had when I was a 'rookie'. They were patient, helpful, and above all, they were encouraging. They encouraged me to achieve things I didn't believe I could achieve. They helped me aim high and that has made all the difference in my life.

Thank you Nancy and Gary

Lack of direction,

not lack of time, is the problem.

We all have

twenty-four hour days.

– Zig Ziglar

The difference between

'TRY'

and

'TRIUMPH'

is just a little *'UMPH!'*

– Marvin Phillips

A smart salesperson listens to emotions not facts.

~Unknown

Good ideas are common

– what's uncommon are people who will work hard enough to bring them about.

~Ashleigh Brilliant

FALLING DOWN IS HOW WE GROW.

STAYING DOWN IS HOW WE DIE.

~Brian Vaszily

Always be closing...

That doesn't mean you're always closing the deal,

but it does mean that you need to be always closing on the next step in the process.

Shane Gibson

Success seems to be connected with action.

Successful people keep moving.

They make mistakes, but they don't quit.

~ Conrad Hilton

If you are going to achieve excellence in **big** things, you develop the habit in **little** matters.

Excellence is not an exception, it is a prevailing attitude.

– Charles R. Swindoll

Success is not the key to happiness.

Happiness is the key to success.

If you love what you are doing, you will be successful.

–Albert Schweitzer

It is hard to fail,

but it is worse never to have tried to succeed

 -Theodore Roosevelt

Act now.

There is never any time but **now**,

and there never will be any time but now.

–Wallace Wattles

There are those who work all day.

Those who dream all day.

And those who spend an hour dreaming before setting to work to fulfill those dreams.

Go into the third category because there's virtually no competition.

– Steven J Ross

The tragedy of life doesn't lie in not reaching your goal.

The tragedy lies in having no goals to reach.

– Benjamin Mays

If you don't design your own life plan, chances are you'll fall into someone else's plan.

And guess what they have planned for you?

Not much.

– Jim Rohn

Nothing in the world can take the place of Persistence.

Talent will not; nothing is more common than unsuccessful men with talent.

Genius will not; unrewarded genius is almost a proverb.

Education will not; the world is full of educated derelicts.

Persistence and determination alone are omnipotent.

The slogan 'Press On' has solved and always will solve the problems of the human race.

–Calvin Coolidge

Successful and unsucessful people do not vary greatly in their abilities.

They vary in their desires to reach their potential.

–John Maxwell

You need to be aware of what others are doing,

applaud their efforts,

acknowledge their successes, and encourage them in their pursuits.

When we all help one another, everybody wins.

– Jim Stovall

Try a thing you haven't done three times.

Once, to get over the fear of doing it.

Twice, to learn how to do it.

And a **third** time to figure out whether you like it or not.

-Virgil Thomson

Use what talents you possess,

the woods will be very silent if no birds sang there except those that sang best.

– Henry van Dyke

Always do your best.

What you plant now, you will harvest later.

- Og Mandino

Today is always the most productive day of your week.

– Mark Hunter

If your work is becoming uninteresting, so are you.

Work is an inanimate thing and can be made lively and interesting only by injecting yourself into it.

Your job is only as big as you are.

– George C. Hubbs

It is not your customer's job to remember **you**.

It is your obligation and responsibility to make sure they don't have the chance to forget you.

– Patricia Fripp

Here is a simple but powerful rule ... always give people more than they expect to get.

– Nelson Boswell

Obstacles don't have to stop you. If you run into a wall, don't turn around and give up.

Figure out how to climb it, go through it, or work around it.

– Michael Jordan

It is amazing what you can accomplish if you do not care who gets the credit.

– Harry Truman

Today I will do what others won't,

so **tomorrow** I can accomplish what others can't.

– Jerry Rice

I've learned that people will forget what you said,

people will forget what you did,

but people will **<u>never</u>** forget how you made them feel.

– Maya Angelou

You can't build a reputation on what you're *going* to do.

– Henry Ford

To succeed in sales, simply talk to lots of people every day.

And here's what's **exciting**- there are lots of people!

-Jim Rohn

Remember that failure is an event, not a person.

Yesterday ended last night.

- Zig Ziglar

Pretend that every single person you meet has a sign around his or her neck that says,

'Make me feel important.'

Not only will you succeed in sales, you will succeed in life.

– Mary Kay Ash

How you think when you lose determines how long it will be until you win.

– Gilbert K. Chesterton

If you are not taking care of your customer, your competitor will.

– Bob Hooey

Opportunities are usually disguised as hard work, so most people don't recognize them.

– Ann Landers

Formal education will make you a living;

self-education will make you a fortune.

- Jim Rohn

You are your greatest asset.

Put your time, effort and money into training, grooming, and encouraging your greatest asset.

Tom Hopkins

People who are unable to motivate themselves must be content with mediocrity, no matter how impressive their other talents.

Andrew Carnegie

If you have no confidence in self, you are twice defeated in the race of life.

With confidence, you have won even before you have started.

Cicero

It is not the strongest of the species that survives,

nor the most intelligent that survives.

It is the one that is the most <u>adaptable to change</u>.

Charles Darwin

You've got to be success minded.

You've got to feel that things are coming your way when you're out selling; otherwise, you won't be able to sell anything.

Curtis Carlson

A successful man is one who can lay a firm foundation with the bricks others have thrown at him.

David Brinkley

The best way to appreciate your job is to imagine yourself without one.

Oscar Wilde

If you aren't fired
with enthusiasm,

you will be fired with
enthusiasm.

-Vince Lombardi

When one door closes,

another opens,

but we often look so long and
so regretfully upon the closed
door that we do not see the
one which has opened for us.

-Alexander Graham Bell

Too many people miss the silver lining because they're expecting gold.

-Maurice Setter

You are never too old to set another goal or to dream a new dream.

-C.S. Lewis

Nothing is particularly hard if you divide it into small jobs.

-Henry Ford

Nothing can add more power to your life than concentrating all of your energies on a limited set of targets.

-*Nido Qubein*

The pessimist complains about the wind.

The optimist expects it to change.

The leader adjusts the sails.

-John Maxwell

Don't be afraid to take a **big step** if one is indicated.

You can't cross a chasm in two small jumps.

-David Lloyd George

You'll never be a loser until you quit trying.

-Mike Ditka

ALWAYS DO MORE THAN IS REQUIRED OF YOU.

-General George S. Patton

This book was supposed to have 52 sayings, but I gave you 53...always do more!